# Manners are Magical

By Susan Livingston

Illustrated by Barb Zeien Togneri    Design by Lori Korte Design

For Anney and Patrick

S. L.

To our darling Quinn,
    Sorry we couldn't celebrate your 4th birthday with you. You are so special to us and always in our hearts. We love you so much. Grandma knows the woman that illustrated (drew the pictures) this book. In fact she used to baby-sit me. Isn't that a funny story? Have fun spending your birthday money. Let us know what you buy for yourself.
        Love,
        Grandma & Grandpa Hanson

Text copyright © 2007 by Susan Livingston
Illustrations copyright © 2007 by Barb Zeien Togneri
All rights reserved. Unless otherwise noted, no part of this book may be reproduced, stored in a retrieval system, or transmitted in any form or by any means, electronic, mechanical, photocopying, recording or otherwise, without express written permission of the publisher, except for brief quotations or critical reviews.
Printed in the USA
Book design by Lori Korte Design

The text is set in Monotype Corisva and Bell MT.
Illustrations are rendered in colored pencil.

Did you know that

Manners are *Magical?*

Well they are!

Manners are magical because when you use good manners
you are treating others with kindness and respect,
AND
when you treat others with kindness
and respect, special things will happen....

You will get along better with others,

you will make friends more easily,

you will help others to feel good about themselves, and

you will feel good about yourself, too.

Now that's *Magical!*

Are you wondering what these manners are?
You probably know some of them already.
Let's begin with the famous
MAGIC WORDS.
See if you can guess what they are
before you turn the page.

Ta Dah! Here they are.
The amazing MAGIC WORDS!
Were you able to guess some of them?

The magic words are only the beginning. Read on as we present more magical manners that you can practice so special things will happen for you!

## SMILE A LOT.

When you greet, meet, or speak to others,
light up your face with a smile.

## WELCOME OTHERS.

When you play, eat lunch, or when
you are just hanging around, welcome others
so they don't feel left out.

## HELP OTHERS.

When someone looks stuck
or a little mixed up, offer a helping hand!

## GIVE COMPLIMENTS.

When you like someone's look
or the way they do things,
go ahead and let them know!

## STICK UP FOR EACH OTHER.

Being teased or picked on hurts feelings.
If it's safe, stick up for others,
OR ask an adult for help!

# SHARE.

If you have extras be sure to share,
and let others join in on the fun.

# You can also SHARE by taking turns...

...or by trading.

## COOPERATE WHEN YOU PLAY.

It's amazing what you can
do with a little teamwork.

"This is looking great. We all pitched in."

# LISTEN WELL.

When others are talking, listen with your ears, look at them with your eyes, and keep your body still.

"I went camping last weekend with my family. We slept in a tent. I had a great time!"

Be sure not to interrupt while others are talking.

INSTEAD of interrupting...

Wait quietly for a pause and say, "excuse me," or wait until the speaker has finished talking before you speak.

## "JUST SAY NO" TO GOSSIPING.

Saying unkind things about others is never a good idea. It's called gossiping, and it hurts others' feelings. You can help stop gossiping by not joining in, or by saying something nice about the person.

# USE YOUR MOST *FABULOUS* TABLE MANNERS.

Don't forget to chew with your mouth closed, and be sure to finish your food before you speak!

"Did you see Lion's great catch during recess? He saved the game!"

# GIVE EACH OTHER SPACE.

It does not feel good when others move in *soooo* close.
Unless you know it is okay, better to stay an arms length away!

"Want to play catch at recess?"   "Yes, but would you please not get so close. I'm trying to read"

That's more like it.

# SAY, "GO AHEAD" OR "AFTER YOU"

Rushing to the head of the line or budging hurts feelings and sometimes bodies. Say "go ahead" or "after you" and see what these special words will do!

We hope you have enjoyed the manners we have shared with you! Now we invite you to practice these manners, so special things will happen, and you will see why........

## A Note To Teachers and Parents

A lot of attention has been given to the problem of bullying in schools, and rightly so. Generally bullying curriculums are tailored to address students in third grade on through high school. There is a golden opportunity here that should not be missed, namely to teach good manners to children from pre-k on through the second grade. Teaching good manners is a proactive approach which can help to prevent bullying behaviors in the future. Good manners help us to get along with others, by being kind, considerate and respectful. Good manners help to build a strong supportive sense of community. Strong supportive communities tolerate differences in one another, and discourage bullying behaviors. Schools in partnership with parents have the chance to teach our young children good manners which will inevitably discourage both bullying behaviors which go against the code of good manners and will discourage tolerance of bullying behaviors which go against the very nature of strong supportive communities.

## Activities and Discussion Starters

- Beginning with "Use Your Magic Words", feature each of the manners as the "Manner of the Week". Ask students to practice using the Manner of the Week and to notice when others practice the manner, taking note of how it feels when others practice or do not practice the particular manner.

- Divide students into small groups and have them role play the Manner of the Week in a skit. Have students present their skits and invite reactions and/or comments.

- Teach students how to sign the magic words (see examples at right).

- Discuss television shows that students like, and talk about the characters' manners. Who has good manners and who has poor manners?

- Have students create their own manners book. As you study each "Manner of the Week", hand out coloring pages with the manner written on the bottom of the page. Ask students to illustrate the manner. Collate once each manner has been illustrated.

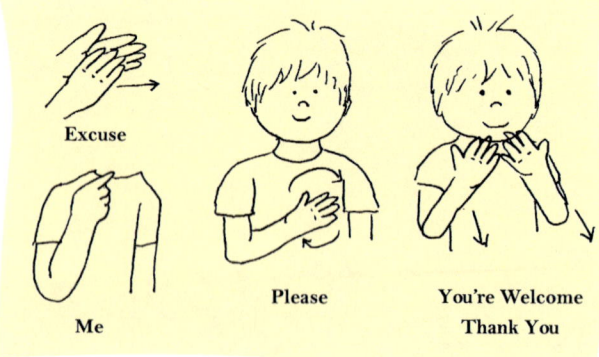

- Partner with parents so they know what manners their children are learning, and can reinforce learning at home by practicing the manners with their children!

## Sample Letter

*Dear Parents,*

*This week and throughout the year we will be talking about manners ("Manners are Magical").*

*Being polite and respectful are part of being a good friend and a good citizen.*

*This week your child will be learning the magic words of manners: please, thank you, sorry, your welcome... and how they make people feel.*

*You can help your child by reinforcing these magic words at home. When you hear them using these words or see them being polite and respectful, praise your child. Tell them you are proud to hear these "magic words" coming from them.*

*Attached are some of our magic words in sign language. You can use these with your child and have a little fun learning another language!*

## About the Author and Illustrator

SUSAN LIVINGSTON, M.S. in Counseling education, is a school counselor at St. Thomas More School, K-8. She lives with her family in St. Paul.

BARB ZEIEN TOGNERI is a freelance artist with a B.S. in Child Development, and an M.S. in Parent Education. Barb loves traveling and enjoying people wherever she goes. Barb's husband, John, is also a fellow artist from Scotland who she met on one of her journeys. They reside in St. Paul, Minnesota.

## Additional Books for Children

*My Manners Matter*
*A First Look at Being Polite*
Pat Thomas
(Barrons, 2006)

*Oops! The Manners Guide for Girls*
Nancy Holyoke, Debbie Tilley
(American Girl Library, Pleasant Company Publishing, 1997)

*Manners Can Be Fun*
Munro Leaf
(Universe Publishing, 2004)

*Time to Say "Please"!*
Mo Williams
(Hyperion Books for Children, 2005)

*The Guide to Good Manners for Kids*
Peggy Post, Cindy Post Senning, Ed.D
(Harper Collins Publishers, 2004)

*How to Lose All Your Friends*
Nancy Carlson
(New York: Puffin, 1997)

*How to Be a Friend*
Laurie Kransy Brown, Marc Brown
(Boston: Little, Brown & Company, 1998)

Made in the USA
Middletown, DE
29 November 2021

53692612R00027